ELON MUSK

THE FOUNDER OF TESLA, PAYPAL, AND SPACE X

By K. Connors

CW01425631

Table of Contents

INTRODUCTION

Elon Musk is one of the greatest and most prolific modern inventors and is responsible for monumental advancements in futuristic technology like renewable energy and space travel. Many of his innovations seem to be right out of a science-fiction movie, but throughout his career, he has discovered huge scientific breakthroughs. After making his first fortune from the internet payment service 'PayPal', he invested $100 million in his space travel company, 'SpaceX'. He began building satellites, launch vehicles, and other spacecraft both for NASA and for his own company, creating new milestones with his privately-funded spacecraft. Many of his revolutionary ideas and inventions focus on space travel, renewable energy, commercial electric cars, and other technologies that look to a future where fossil fuels and other resources may be in shorter supply. His futuristic and visionary ideas have won him both scientific and philanthropic recognition and awards. Pop culture sometimes portrays him as a real-life superhero, dedicated to providing worldwide solutions to international problems.

Musk looks to the future, hopes for intelligent life elsewhere in the universe and continues to plan far-reaching futuristic goals such as a human colony on Mars.

CHAPTER ONE

CHILDHOOD AND FAMILY

Elon Musk grew up in a normal environment just like us, but what makes him different is that he has always been fond of using and exploring the wonders of technology. He purchased his very first company when he was just 10 years old and decided to start programming. In fact just two years after that, he was able to create Blastar, his very first game, and made it available for purchase.

Elon Musk is a South African entrepreneur who became a US citizen in 2002. Elon Musk is known for founding Tesla Motors and SpaceX, which launched a landmark commercial spacecraft in 2012.

Musk is the oldest of three siblings with a prodigious family name; he grew up in the last decades of the Apartheid.

His parents were Maye Musk, a British-Canadian model and Errol Musk, a South Africa-born British electrical engineer. When they divorced in 1980, Elon stayed with his father in South Africa.

EDUCATION

At age 17, in 1989, Elon Musk moved to Canada to attend Queen's University, to avoid mandatory service in the South African military. He left in 1992 to study business and physics at the University of Pennsylvania. He graduated with an undergraduate degree in economics and stayed for a second bachelor's degree in physics.

After leaving Penn, Elon Musk headed to Stanford University in California to pursue a Ph.D. in energy physics. However, his move timed perfectly with the Internet boom, and he dropped out of Stanford after just two days to become a part of it, launching his first company, Zip2 Corporation.

As an online city guide, Zip2 was soon providing content for the new websites of both The New York Times and the Chicago Tribune. In 1999, a division of Compaq Computer Corporation bought Zip2 for $307 million in cash and $34 million in stock options.

In addition to the bachelor's degrees that he earned in physics and economics, he also holds an honorary doctorate in Design from the 'Art Center College of Design' and an honorary doctorate in Aerospace Engineering from the 'University of Surrey'.

ELON MUSK'S COMPANIES

1. PAYPAL

In 1999, Musk co-founded X.com, an online financial services/payments company. An X.com accusation the following year led to the creation of PayPal as it is known today, and in October 2002, PayPal was acquired by eBay for $1.5 billion in stock. Before the sale, Musk owned 11 percent of PayPal's stock.

2. FOUNDER OF SPACE X

Musk founded his third company, Space Exploration Technologies Corporation, or SpaceX, in 2002 with the intention of building spacecraft for commercial space travel. By 2008, SpaceX was well established, and NASA awarded SpaceX the contract to handle cargo transport for the International Space Station—with plans for astronaut transport in the future—in a move to replace NASA's own space shuttle missions.

3. FALCON 9 ROCKETS

On May 22, 2012, Musk and SpaceX made history when the company launched its Falcon 9 rocket into space with an unmanned capsule. The vehicle was sent to the International Space Station with 1,000 pounds of supplies for the astronauts stationed there, marking this the first time that a private company had sent a spacecraft to the International Space Station. Of the launch, Musk was quoted as saying, "I feel very lucky, for us, it's like winning the Super Bowl."

In December 2013, SpaceX accomplished another milestone when Falcon 9 carried a satellite in to geosynchronous transfer orbit, a distance at which the satellite would lock into an orbital path that matched the Earth's rotation. In February 2015, SpaceX launched another Falcon 9 fitted with the Deep Space Climate Observatory (DSCOVR) satellite, aiming to observe the extreme emissions from the sun that affect power grids and communications systems on Earth.

In March 2017, SpaceX enjoyed another breakthrough with the successful test flight and landing of a Falcon 9 rocket made from reusable parts. This development opened the door for more affordable space travel. A setback came in November 2017, when an explosion occurred during a test of the company's new Block 5 Merlin engine. SpaceX reported that no one was injured and that the issue would not hamper its planned rollout of a future generation of Falcon 9 rockets.

4.   FOUNDER & CEO OF TESLA

Elon Musk is the co-founder, CEO and product architect at Tesla Motors, a company dedicated to producing affordable, mass-market electric cars as well as battery products and solar roofs. Musk oversees all product development, engineering, and design of the company's products. Five years after its formation in 2008, the company unveiled the Roadster, a sports car capable of accelerating from 0 to 60 mph in 3.7 seconds, as well traveling nearly 250 miles between charges of its lithium-ion battery. With a stake in the company taken by Daimler and a strategic partnership with Toyota, Tesla Motors launched its initial public offering in June 2010, raising $226 million.

Additional successes include the Model S, the company's first electric sedan. Capable of covering 265 miles between charges. The Model S was honored as the 2013 Car of the Year by Motor Trend magazine.

In April 2017, Tesla announced that it surpassed General Motors to become the most valuable U.S. car maker. The news was an obvious boon to Tesla, which was looking to ramp up production and released its Model 3 sedan later that year.

In November 2017, Musk made another splash with the unveiling of the new Tesla Semi and Roadster at the company's design studio.

The semi truck, which enters into production in 2019, boasts 500 miles of range as well as a battery and motors built to last 1 million miles. The Roadster, set to follow in 2020, will become the fastest production car ever made with its 0 to 60 times in 1.9 seconds.

"The point of doing this is to just give a hardcore smack-down to gasoline cars," Musk told the crowd. "Driving a gasoline sports car is going to feel like a steam engine with a side of quiche."

After initially aiming to produce 5,000 new Model 3 cars per week by December 2017, Musk pushed that goal back to March 2018, and then to June with the start of the new year. The announced delay didn't surprise industry experts, who were well aware of the company's production problems, although some questioned how long the investors would remain patient with the process.

In January 2018, Tesla announced a radical new compensation package for its CEO, in which Musk would be paid only if he reached milestones of growing valuation based on $50 billion increments. At the top end of that chart, if Tesla reached a company value of $650 billion, then Musk stood to benefit from a stock award worth as much as $55 billion.

5.   SOLARCITY ACQUISITION

In August 2016, in Musk's continuing effort to promote and advance sustainable energy and products for a wider consumer base, a $2.6 billion dollar deal was solidified to combine his electric car and solar energy companies. Tesla Motors Inc. announced an all-stock deal purchase of SolarCity Corp., a company Musk had helped his cousins start in 2006. He is a majority shareholder in each entity.

"Solar and storage are at their best when they're combined. As one company, Tesla (storage) and SolarCity (solar) can create fully integrated residential, commercial and grid-scale products that improve the way that energy is generated, stored and consumed,"

The companies listed above are just some of the companies that he has invested in. Apart from that, he has also invested in many of other things. Some have failed while some have become extremely successful. He was always willing to take a risk and that has paved the way for him to become a billionaire.

For him, technology is not the only thing that matters for people are important in this world. In fact, he has also been very active in doing charitable works and has even created his own foundation while supporting others as well. This is the secret of his success, the success that he is still enjoying up to this day.

OTHER INVENTIONS & INNOVATIONS

Outside of his roles at SpaceX and Tesla, Musk has continually attempted to make his innovative ideas a reality.

HYPERLOOP

In August 2013, Elon Musk released a concept for a new form of transportation called the "Hyperloop," an invention that would foster commuting between major cities while severely cutting travel time. Ideally resistant to weather and powered by renewable energy, the Hyperloop would propel riders in pods through a network of low-pressure tubes at speeds reaching more than 700 mph. Musk noted that the Hyperloop could take from seven to ten years to be built and ready for use.

He introduced the Hyperloop with claims that it would be safer than a plane or train, with an estimated cost of $6 billion. This is approximately one-tenth of the cost for the rail system planned by the state of California. However, Musk's concept has drawn skepticism. Nevertheless, the entrepreneur has sought to encourage the development of this idea. After he announced a competition for teams to submit their designs for a Hyperloop pod prototype, the first Hyperloop Pod Competition was held at the SpaceX facility in January 2017.

OpenAI

Elon Musk has pursued an interest in Artificial Intelligence, becoming co-chair of the nonprofit OpenAI. The research company launched in late 2015 with the stated mission of advancing digital intelligence to benefit humanity. In 2017, it was also revealed that Musk was backing a venture called Neuralink, which intends to create devices to be implanted in the human brain and help people merge with software.

BORING COMPANY

In yet another innovation, in January 2017 Elon Musk suddenly decided he was going find a way to reduce traffic by devoting resources to boring and building tunnels. He launched his venture, named "The Boring Company", with a test dig on the SpaceX property in Los Angeles. In late October, Musk posted the first photo of his company's progress to his Instagram page.

He said that the 500-foot tunnel, which would generally run parallel to Interstate 405 would reach a length of two miles in approximately four months.

HIGH-SPEED TRAIN

In late November 2017, after Chicago Mayor Rahm Emanuel asked for proposals to build and operate a high-speed rail line that would transport passengers from O'Hare Airport to downtown Chicago in 20 minutes or less, Musk tweeted that he was all-in on the competition with his Boring Company. He said that the concept of the Chicago loop would be different from his Hyperloop, with its relatively short route not requiring the need for drawing a vacuum to eliminate air friction.

PERSONAL LIFE & LEGACY

Elon Musk has married three times and twice to the same woman. His first marriage was to Canadian author Justine Wilson in 2000. They had six children together: all sons. Their first son, Nevada Alexander Musk, died at the age of 10 weeks.

The couple had five more sons through IVF; twins in 2004, followed by triplets in 2006. Elon Musk and Justine Wilson divorced in 2008.

In 2008, he began dating English actress, Talulah Riley, and the two of them got married in 2010. The couple separated in 2012.

In 2013, Elon Musk remarried Talulah Riley but the couple filed for divorce in 2014 and it was finalized in 2016.

Elon Musk was briefly in a relationship with American actress Amber Heard in 2016 but the couple split owing to their conflicting schedules.

NET WORTH

As of December 2017, Elon Musk's net worth is $20.2 billion according to Forbes. He earned his first billion with the sale of PayPal in 2002. His company SpaceX is valued at more than $20 billion.

AWARDS & ACHIEVEMENTS

In 2010, the premier world organization for aerospace records, the 'Federation Aéronautique Internationale' awarded Musk the 'FAI Gold Space Medal. He shares this honor with prominent personalities like Neil Armstrong and John Glenn.

He has won multiple awards and recognition for his many advancements in science, technology and business alike and in 2013, he was named 'Fortune' magazine's 'Businessperson of the Year' for his companies 'SpaceX', 'Tesla Motors' and 'SolarCity'

In 2016, he was ranked 21st on the Forbes list of The World's Most Powerful People.

He was ranked 21st wealthiest person in America in the 2017 Forbes 400 list.

TRUMP ADVISER

With Donald Trump announcing plans to pursue massive infrastructure developments after his successful election to the U.S. presidency in 2016, Musk found himself on common ground with the new president and his advisers. That December, he was named to President Trump's Strategy and Policy Forum, and the following January, he joined Trump's Manufacturing Jobs Initiative.

While sometimes at odds with the president's controversial measures, such as a proposed ban on immigrants from Muslim-majority countries, Musk defended his involvement with the new administration. "My goals," he tweeted in early 2017, "are to accelerate the world's transition to sustainable energy and to help make humanity a multi-planet civilization, a consequence of which will be the creating of hundreds of thousands of jobs and a more inspiring future for all."

On June 1, following Trump's announcement that he was withdrawing the U.S. from the Paris climate accord, Musk stepped down from his advisory roles.

NON-PROFIT

The boundless potential of space exploration and the preservation of the future of the human race have become the cornerstones of Musk's abiding interests, and toward these, he has founded the Musk Foundation, which is dedicated to space exploration and the discovery of renewable and clean energy sources.

CHAPTER TWO

DAYS IN CANADA AND AFRICA

In 1988, a 19-year-old Elon Musk moved from South Africa to Canada, hoping to one day emigrate to the United States.

Musk's great escape to Canada was not well thought out. He knew of a great-uncle in Montreal, hopped on a flight and hoped for the best. Upon landing in June 1988, Musk found a pay phone and tried to use directory assistance to find his uncle. When that didn't work, he called his mother to collect his uncle. She had bad news. Maye had sent a letter to the uncle in question before Musk left and had received a reply while her son was in transit. The uncle had gone to Minnesota, meaning that Musk had nowhere to stay. Bags in hand, Musk headed for a youth hostel.

After spending a few days in Montreal exploring the city, Musk tried to come up with a long-term plan. Maye had family scattered all across Canada and Musk began reaching out to them.

He bought a countrywide bus ticket that let him hop on and off as he pleased for one hundred dollars and opted to head to Saskatchewan, the former home of his grandfather. After a 1,900-mile bus ride, he ended up in Swift Current, a town of fifteen thousand people. Musk called his second cousin out of the blue from the bus station and hitched a ride to his house.

Musk spent the next year working a series of odd jobs around Canada. He tended vegetables and shoveled out grain bins at a cousin's farm located in the tiny town of Waldeck. Musk celebrated his eighteenth birthday there, sharing a cake with the family he'd just met and a few strangers from the neighborhood. After that, he learned to cut logs with a chainsaw in Vancouver, British Columbia. The hardest job Musk took came after a visit to the unemployment office. He inquired about the job with the best wage, which turned out to be a gig cleaning the boiler room of a lumber mill for eighteen dollars an hour. "You have to put on this hazmat suit and then shimmy through this little tunnel that you can barely fit in," Musk said.

"Then, you have a shovel, you take the sand, and take out other residue, which is still steaming hot, and you have to shovel it through the same hole you came through. There is no escape. Someone else on the other side has to shovel it into a wheelbarrow. If you stay in there for more than thirty minutes, you get too hot and die." Thirty people started out at the beginning of the week. By the third day, five people were left. At the end of the week, it was just Musk and two other men doing the work.

As Musk made his way around Canada, his brother, sister, and mother were figuring out how to get there as well. When Kimbal [Musk] and Elon eventually reunited in Canada, their headstrong and playful natures bloomed. Elon ended up enrolling at Queen's University in Kingston, Ontario, in 1989. (He picked Queen's over the University of Waterloo because he felt like there were more good looking women at Queen's.) Outside of his studies, Elon would read the newspaper alongside Kimbal, and the two of them would identify interesting people they would like to meet. They then took it in turns cold-calling the people they had picked to ask if they were available to have lunch.

Among the harassed was the head of marketing for the Toronto Blue Jays baseball team, a business writer for the Globe and Mail, and a top executive at the Bank of Nova Scotia, Peter Nicholson. Nicholson remembered the boys' call well. "I was not in the habit of getting out-of-the-blue requests," he said. "I was perfectly prepared to have lunch with a couple of kids that had that kind of gumption." It took six months to get on Nicholson's calendar, but, sure enough, the Musk brothers made a three-hour train ride and showed up on time.

Nicholson's first exposure to the Musk brothers left him with an impression many would share. Both presented themselves well and were polite. Elon clearly came off as the geekier, more awkward counterpoint to the charismatic, personable Kimbal. "I became more impressed and fascinated as I talked to them," Nicholson said. "They were so determined." Nicholson ended up offering Elon a summer internship at the bank and became his trusted advisor.

Not long after their initial meeting, Elon invited Peter Nicholson's daughter Christie to his birthday party.

Christie showed up at Maye's Toronto apartment with a jar of homemade lemon curd in hand and was greeted by Elon and about fifteen other people. Elon had never met Christie before, but he went right up to her and led her to a couch. "Then, I believe the second sentence out of his mouth was "I think a lot about electric cars," Christie said. "And then he turned to me and said, "Do you think about electric cars?" The conversation left Christie, who is now a science writer, with the distinct impression that Musk was handsome, affable and a tremendous nerd. "For whatever reason, I was so struck by that moment on the sofa," she said. "You could tell that this person was very different. He captivated me in that way."

With her angular features and blond hair, Christie fit Musk's type, and the two stayed in touch during Musk's time in Canada. They never really dated, but Christie found Musk interesting enough to have lengthy conversations with him on the phone. "One night he told me, If there was a way that I could not eat, so I could work more, I would not eat. I wish there was a way to get nutrients without sitting down for a meal." The enormity of his work ethic at that age and his intensity jumped out.

"It seemed like one of the more unusual things I had ever heard."

College suited Musk. He worked on being less of a know-it-all, while also finding a group of people who respected his intellectual abilities. The university students were less inclined to laugh off or deride his opinionated takes on energy, space, and whatever else was captivating him in the moment. Musk had found people who responded to his ambition rather than mocking it and he fed on this environment.

Navaid Farooq, a Canadian who grew up in Geneva, ended up in Musk's freshman-year dormitory in the fall of 1990. Both men were placed in the international section where a Canadian student would get paired with a student from overseas. Musk sort of broke the system since he technically counted as a

Canadian but knew almost nothing about his surroundings. "I had a roommate from Hong Kong, and he was a really nice guy," Musk said. "He religiously attended every lecture, which was helpful, since I went to the least number of classes possible." For a time, Musk sold computer parts and full PCs in the dorm to make some extra cash.

"I could build something to suit their needs like a tricked-out gaming machine or a simple word processor that cost less than what they could get in a store," Musk said. "Or if their computer didn't boot properly or had a virus, I'd fix it. I could pretty much solve any problem." Farooq and Musk bonded over their backgrounds living abroad and a shared interest in strategy board games. "I don't think he makes friends easily, but he is very loyal to those he has," Farooq said. When the video game Civilization was released, the college chums spent hours building their empire, much to the dismay of Farooq's girlfriend who was forgotten in another room. "Elon could lose himself for hours on end," Farooq said. The students also relished their loner lifestyles. "We are the kind of people that can be by ourselves at a party and not feel awkward," Farooq said. "We can think to ourselves and not feel socially weird about it."

Musk was more ambitious in college than he'd been in high school. He studied business, competed in public speaking contests, and began to display the brand of intensity and competitiveness that marks his behavior today.

After one economics exam, Musk, Farooq, and some other students in class came back to the dorms and began comparing notes to try to ascertain how well they did on the test. It soon became clear that Musk had a firmer grasp on the material than anyone else. "This was a group of fairly high achievers, and Elon stood way outside of the bell curve," Farooq said. Musk's intensity has continued to be a constant in their long relationship. "When Elon gets into something, he develops just this different level of interest in it than other people. That is what differentiates Elon from the rest of humanity."

In 1992, having spent two years at Queen's, Musk transferred to the University of Pennsylvania on a scholarship. Musk saw the Ivy League school as possibly opening some additional doors and went off in pursuit of dual degrees—first an economics degree from the Wharton School and then a bachelor's degree in physics. Justine stayed at Queen's, pursuing her dream of becoming a writer, and maintained a long-distance relationship with Musk. Now and again, she would visit him, and the two would sometimes head off to New York for a romantic weekend.

Musk blossomed even more at Penn and really started to feel comfortable when hanging out with his fellow physics students. "At Penn, he met people that thought like him," Maye said. "There were some nerds there. He so enjoyed them. I remember going for lunch with them, and they were talking physics things. They would laugh out loud. Once again, however, Musk did not make many friends among the broader school body. It's difficult to find former students who remember him being there at all. But he did make one very close friend named Adeo Ressi, who would go on to be a Silicon Valley entrepreneur in his own right. To this day Adeo is close to Elon as anyone.

Ressi was a lanky guy well over six feet tall and possessed an eccentric air. He was the artistic, colorful foil to the studious, more buttoned-up than Musk. Both of the young men were transfer students and ended up being placed in the funky freshman dorm. The lackluster social scene did not live up to Ressi's expectations, and he talked Musk into renting a large house off campus. They got the ten-bedroom home relatively cheap since it was a frat house that had gone unrented.

During the week, Musk and Ressi would study but as the weekend approached, Ressi in particular would transform the house into a nightclub. He covered the windows with trash bags to make it pitch black inside and decorated the walls with bright paints and whatever objects he could find. "It was a full-out, unlicensed speakeasy," Ressi said. "We would have as many as five hundred people. We would charge five dollars, and it would be pretty much all you could drink; beer and Jell-O shots and other things."

Come Friday night, the ground around the house would shake from the intensity of the bass being pumped out by Ressi's speakers. Maye visited one of the parties and discovered that Ressi had hammered objects into the walls and lacquered them with glow-in-the-dark paint. She ended up working the door as the coat check/money taker and grabbed a pair of scissors for protection as the cash piled up in a shoe box.

A second house had fourteen rooms. Musk, Ressi, and one other person lived there. They fashioned tables by laying plywood on top of used kegs and came up with other makeshift furniture ideas.

Musk returned home one day to find that Ressi had nailed his desk to the wall and then painted it in Day-Glo colors. Musk retaliated by pulling his desk down, painting it black, and studying. "I'm like, Dude, that's installation art in our party house," said Ressi. Remind Musk of this incident and he'll respond matter-of-factly, "It was a desk."

Musk will still have the occasional vodka and Diet Coke, but he's not a big drinker and does not really care for the taste of alcohol. "Somebody had to stay sober during these parties," Musk said. "I was paying my own way through college and could make an entire month's rent in one night. Adeo was in charge of doing cool shit around the house, and I would run the party." As Ressi put it, "Elon was the most straight-laced dude you have ever met. He never drank. He never did anything. Zero. Literally nothing." The only time Ressi had to step in and moderate Musk's behavior came during the video game binges that could go on for days.

Musk's longtime interest in solar power and in finding other new ways to harness energy expanded while he was at Penn. In December 1994, he had to come up with a business plan for one of his classes and ended up writing a paper titled "The Importance of Being Solar." The document started with a bit of Musk's wry sense of humor. At the top of the page, he wrote: "The sun will come out tomorrow." Little Orphan Annie on the subject of renewable energy. The paper went on to predict a rise in solar power technology based on material improvements and the construction of large scale solar plants. Musk delved deeply into how solar cells work and the various compounds that can make them more efficient. He concluded the paper with a drawing of the "power station of the future." It depicted a pair of giant solar arrays in space, every four kilometers in width, sending their juice down to Earth via microwave beams to a receiving antenna with a seven-kilometer diameter. Musk received a 98 on what his professor deemed a "very interesting and well-written paper."

A second paper talked about taking research documents and books, electronically scanning them, performing optical character recognition, and putting all of the information in to a single database—much like a mix between today's Google Books and Google Scholar. A third paper dwelled on another of Musk's favorite topics—ultracapacitors.

In the forty-four-page document, Musk is plainly jubilant over the idea of a new form of energy storage that would suit his future pursuits with cars, planes, and rockets. Pointing to the latest research coming out of a lab in Silicon Valley, he wrote: "The end result represents the first new means of storing significant amounts of electrical energy since the development of the battery and fuel cell. Furthermore, because the Ultracapacitor retains the basic properties of a capacitor, it can deliver its energy over one hundred times faster than a battery of equivalent weight, and be recharged just as quickly." Musk received a 97 for this effort and praise for "a very thorough analysis" with "excellent financials!"

The remarks from the professor were spot-on. Musk's clear, concise, writing is the work of a logician, moving from one point to the next with precision. What truly stood out though, was Musk's ability to master difficult physics concepts in the midst of actual business plans. Even then, he showed an unusual knack for being able to perceive a path from a scientific advance to a for-profit enterprise.

As Musk began to think more seriously about what he would do after college, he briefly considered getting into the video game business. He'd been obsessed with video games since his childhood and had held a gaming internship. But he came to see them as not quite grand enough of a pursuit. "I really like computer games, but then if I made really great computer games, how much effect would that have on the world," he said. "It wouldn't have a big effect. Even though I have an intrinsic love of video games, I couldn't bring myself to do that as a career."

In interviews, Musk often makes sure that people know that he had some truly big ideas on his mind during this period of his life.

As he tells it, he would daydream at Queen's and Penn and usually end up with the same conclusion. He viewed the Internet, renewable energy, and space as the three areas that would undergo significant change in the years to come and the markets where he could make a big impact. He vowed to pursue projects in all three. "I told all my ex-girlfriends and my ex-wife about these ideas," he said. "It probably sounded like super-crazy talk."

Musk's insistence on explaining the early origins of his passion for electric cars, solar energy, and rockets can come off as an insecurity. It feels as if Musk is trying to shape his life story in a forced way.

But for Musk, the distinction between stumbling into something and having intent is important. Musk has long wanted the world to know that he's different from the run-of-the-mill entrepreneurs in Silicon Valley. He wasn't just sniffing out trends, and he wasn't consumed by the idea of getting rich. He'd been in pursuit of a master plan all along. "I really was thinking about this stuff in college," he said. "It is not some invented story after the fact. I don't want to seem like a Johnny-come-lately or that I'm chasing a fad or just being opportunistic."

"I'm not an investor. I like to make technologies real that I think are important for the future and used in some sort of way."

Excerpted from Elon Musk: Tesla, SpaceX, and the Quest for a Fantastic Future.

CHAPTER THREE

MUSK'S GRAND VISION

The first master plan that Elon Musk wrote 10 years ago is now in the final stages of completion. It wasn't all that complicated and consisted of:

1. Create stunning solar roofs with seamlessly integrated battery storage

2. Expand the electric vehicle product line to address all major segments

3. Develop a self-driving capability that is 10X safer than manual via massive fleet learning

4. Enable your car to make money for you when you aren't using it

FUN FACTS ABOUT ELON MUSK

1. Elon's great-grandma was the first female chiropractor in Canada.

That's not the only odd first in his family.

His grandparents were the first to fly from South Africa to Australia in a single-engine plane. His grandpa won a race from Cape Town to Algiers.

2. Elon read four to five hours a day as a kid.

By the time he was 10, Musk read twice as much as the average for his age. The information that came in one ear stayed there. Musk could blurt out that the moon was 384,400 miles from Earth, on average.

3. The Hitchhiker's Guide to the Galaxy enlightened him.

The book taught him that figuring out the right questions is difficult and that everything else is easy. To discover what questions to ask, Elon believes that society should increase the "scope and scale of human consciousness."

4. Elon was bullied in school.

He was the smallest and youngest guy in his school, and the other children picked on him. His mother said that he was also in conflict with South Africa as a whole. It turned out that he had two recourses.

The first was his family; and his ability to think of himself as a Musk, and therefore as a kind of transcendent citizen rather than as a South African."

5. Despite not having a map, he once tried to bike 50 miles.

Musk grew up in Pretoria, South Africa, which is about 50 miles south of Johannesburg. When he was still young, Elon and his even-younger brother tried to ride their bikes to Johannesburg. The two got lost and somehow made it through "some super-dangerous areas" without harm. Too bad he didn't have a hyperloop yet.

6. Elon also created homemade explosives and fireworks.

Yet still no harm came to him. "It is remarkable how many things you can explode," Elon said. "I'm lucky I have all my fingers." And you thought your illegal M80s were cool.

7. Elon copped his first computer at age 10.

Then he taught himself how to program it. Musk sold his first piece of software, a game called Blastar, two years later for $500.

8. He tried opening an arcade when he was 16.

Elon and his younger brother Kimbal had a lease and suppliers, but the city wouldn't approve their business. Their parents had no idea until afterwards.

9. Elon moved to Canada to make immigrating to the U.S. easier.

After high school, Musk figured out that it would be easier to become an American citizen as a Canadian than a South African. Elon studied at Queens University in Ontario, and in 1992 switched to Penn, where he graduated with degrees in both economics and physics. However, he didn't take the oath of American citizenship until 2002.

10. Elon worked at a lumber mill and cleaned boilers that were so filthy that he needed a hazmat suit.

He didn't jump off the plane and immediately into college. After moving to Canada, Elon was broke and homeless, so he popped up on distant relative's doorsteps and did odd jobs until he could go to school.

11. At Penn, he paid his way through school by throwing house parties.

His roommate made art installations to make their place feel like a club, while Elon handled the business end. The two once got into an intense argument when Musk converted one of his roommate's pieces in to a desk. To this day, they still disagree on whether the piece was art or a piece of furniture.

12. He has been interested in the internet, sustainable energy, and space exploration since college.

Musk said that he has always wanted to create a significant, positive effect on the future of humanity. Right now, you can thank him for making it possible to pay for those Js on eBay or to drive an electric car that doesn't make you look soft. Soon, you can thank him from space.

13. Musk bored his dates with rants about electric cars.

Electric cars don't seem so boring now, do they? Your loss, ladies.

14. He dropped out of Stanford 48 hours after beginning the physics doctoral program.

But he didn't retreat to his parents' basement. Musk launched his first company Zip2, which made an Internet city guide for newspapers including the New York Times and Chicago Tribune. The money that he made from selling the company led him to his involvement with PayPal.

15. Elon made $180 million as a co-founder of PayPal.

He sold the company back in '02. Six million (and 300,000) of that fortune became Musk's initial investment in Tesla in 2004. Today, PayPal has continued to become stronger than ever. In an eBay earnings report released earlier this year, John Donahoe, eBay Inc's President and CEO said that "eBay mobile finished the year with $13 billion in volume - more than double the prior year - and PayPal mobile handled almost $14 billion in payment volume, more than triple the prior year. In 2013, we expect each to exceed $20 billion." As of Q2 of this year, PayPal has more than 132 million active accounts and is involved in more than 200 markets. 16. He was held at gunpoint by police in Russia.

Musk went to Russia to buy three $7-million-dollar rockets for the company that would later become SpaceX. While he was there, he was pulled over several times and had to bribe the police to move on. The sellers turned out to be equally shady, so Musk decided to build his own rockets.

It just so happens that when he was building the rockets, he decided to use an incredible 3D technology with CAD, which meant that he could manipulate the Merlin engines by motioning with his hands in front of a computer screen.

17. Tony Stark's character in the Iron Man movies was inspired by him.

Director Jon Favreau says that when he began working on the first movie, he had no idea how to make Stark seem real. That's when Robert Downey Jr. told Favreau that the two needed to sit down with Musk. "Downey was right," Favreau wrote. "Elon is a paragon of enthusiasm, good humor, and curiosity - a Renaissance man in an era that needs them." In Iron Man 2, Musk played himself in a brief scene.

18. He was an executive producer on Thank You For Smoking.

You know, just in case anybody was thinking about messing with him like back in his school days. He also tweeted in May that he was thinking about a Thank You For Smoking sequel, which would likely target worldwide pollution concerns.

19. Elon insisted upon selling battery packs to other manufacturers.

Tesla was still struggling back in 2007 and needed new sources of income. Costs for the Roadster, priced at $109,000, soared to $140,000. Musk asked Tesla CTO JB Straubel to build a Smart Car powered by a Tesla battery to show to the Daimler executives. Straubel warned that he'd have to pull engineers from working on the Roadster, but Musk insisted. It paid off when the Smart Car was unveiled and Tesla won a contract to supply Daimler with battery packs and also secured a $50 million investment.

20. Elon reimagined the sedan.

When Musk brought in Mazda designer Franz von Holzhausen to work on the Model S, he told von Holzhausen that he wanted to make a four-door car with seven seats. von Holzhausen replied, "That's an SUV, not a sedan." Once again, Musk insisted and von Holzhausen finished a prototype of the game-changing sedan in 2009. It turns out that ditching the combustible engine created a lot more space.

21. Musk ate froyo with Toyota CEO Akio Toyota.

The two CEOs had a fun-filled day driving the Tesla Roadster through California. Toyota wanted to take not one, but two test drives of the electric sports car. After they were done, the two enjoyed a frozen treat at Musk's SpaceX rocket factory. A month later, Toyota invested $50 million in Tesla. When asked why, Toyota said of Musk: "I love him."

22. Elon paid $42 million for a plant valued at $1 billion.

Before the Model S, Tesla was producing the Roadster in a garage in Menlo Park, Cali, individually putting the cars together one by one. In 2009, Tesla only made 800 of the electric sports cars. With the company looking to expand exponentially, Elon came across a factory run by GM and Toyota that was 5.5 million square feet and had a plastics molding factory, two paint facilities, 1.5 miles of assembly lines, and a 50-megawatt power plant within it. About 450,000 cars were being produced at the plant per year at the time. But a plant that size was far more costly than anything his budget allowed for.

Initially, Musk wasn't even allowed to visit the factory in Fremont, but in 2010, GM pulled out of the plant after having to declare bankruptcy, and Toyota planned to shut down production. Interest in the massive building was low, so Musk was able to get away with paying way lower than what the facility was actually worth. He has since also purchased 35 acres adjacent to the factory for a test track and is currently looking into building a lithium-ion battery mega factory with production "comparable to all lithium-ion production in the world."

23. He works 80-100 hours per week and once almost had a nervous breakdown.

Would you expect anything else from the CEO of two companies and chairman of another? His advice for entrepreneurs: "Work like hell." It hasn't all been good vibes however.

Before all of Musk's recent success, there was a moment in 2008 when he had a huge decision to make about the future of SpaceX and Tesla. To him, they were basically his children, and it had come to a point where he had to choose how to distribute his funds. He could put all of it into one and kill the other or spread the funds to both and risk losing it all. He chose the latter.

"I never thought of myself as someone who could have a nervous breakdown, like, what kind of pussy has a nervous breakdown? But I came damn close," Musk once said in an interview with Business Insider.

24. He sunned Mitt Romney.

In one of his many nonsensical statements during his presidential campaign, Mitt Romney called Tesla a "loser." Musk responded after the election by saying that Romney "was right about the object of that statement, but not the subject."

25. He was annoyed with the traffic on California's I-405, so he donated $50K to a group advocating highway improvements.

He also said that he'd be willing to pay for additional workers to help widen the highway. Much more productive than road rage, right?

ELON MUSK'S FEW QUOTES

1. A lot of my motivation comes from me personally looking at things that don't work well and feeling a bit sad about how it would manifest in the future.

2. I read a lot of comic books as I was growing up, and I think that might have influenced me.

I mean, they're always trying to save the world, with their underpants on the outside or wearing skin-tight iron suits

3. My mentality is that of a samurai. I would rather commit seppuku than fail.

(Musk explaining himself to a potential investor)

3. I need to find a girlfriend. That's why I need to carve out just a little more time. I think maybe even another five to 10; how much time does a woman want a week? Maybe 10 hours? That's kind of the minimum? I don't know.

4. I would like to die on Mars, just not on impact."

5. Both Tesla and SpaceX were very close to dying. SpaceX had our third launch failure. We barely had enough resources to do a fourth, and if that had failed it would have been curtains

6. I think humanity needs to be on the path to becoming a multi-planet species, and establishing life as we know it in more than one place

7. Well, I've got to die somewhere, and where better than Mars? Be pretty cool!

8. If you do the simple math, if somebody else is working 50 hours and you are working 100, you'll get twice as much done in the course of a year as the other company.

9. You are always going to buy the trusted brand unless there's a big difference. A lot of times, an entrepreneur will come up with something that is just slightly better. It can't just be slightly better. It has got to be a lot better.

10. All a company is is a group of people that create a problem or service and so are dependent on how talented or hardworking that group is. The degree to which they are focused cohesively in a good direction will determine the success of a company.

11. When interviewing somebody to work in a company, ask them 'tell me about the problems you worked on and how did you solve them'. If someone was really the person who solved the problems, they'd be able to answer at multiple levels and if they weren't, they'd get stuck.

12. Focus on signal over noise. Are these efforts that people are undergoing resulting in a better product or service? If they are not, stop those efforts.

13. If something is important enough, you should try even if the probable outcome is failure.

14. Take risks now and do something bold. You won't regret it.

15. We're doing these things which seem unlikely to succeed and we've been fortunate that at least thus far, they have succeeded.

16. It's really important to like what you do if you don't like it. Life is too short.

17. I'd have to be dead or completely incapacitated to give up.

CHAPTER FOUR

RULES FOR SUCCESS

Elon Musk has been in the spotlight for having a successful professional career. He has been interviewed and invited to speak on several different occasions and at many different venues. He shares many of his ideas and principles, but some rules more frequently than others. Here is the top ten that have helped him to become one of the most influential people of our time.

1. Never give up

Elon Musk, as an entrepreneur, has also had his share of setbacks. SpaceX experienced failures on its mission to resupply the ISS. A rocket failure that exploded after a launch destroyed a cargo capsule intended for the space station. However, this did not stop him from continuing what he envisioned his company to be and what it aims to provide. Today, his company is the largest private producer of rocket engines in the world. It has received contracts from NASA to develop US astronaut transport capability.

2. Really like what you do

He suggests going into a profession, career, business or undertaking that one is naturally attracted to. He believes that if a person really likes what he is doing, even though he may suffer failures and setbacks, he will not be easily discouraged. A person who has a genuine interest in a project or field will naturally gravitate towards it, will be focused and will not be easily distracted.

3. Don't listen to the little man

Elon recommends that when people have set their minds to doing something great, they should avoid listening to those who will try to stop them. Some of their friends may try to discourage them out of their own fears. In this case, it is best to stay away from the negative influences that will try to hold people down or minimize their chances of doing great things.

4. Take a risk

He believes that younger people are in the best situation to take bolder risks.

Those who have just graduated from college or those who are just starting with their careers have the best opportunity, simply because they may only need to worry about themselves. As they grow older and have a family, they now have to consider other people that may be affected by their decisions.

5. Do something important

When Elon invested in Tesla, he was not entirely sure that the company would succeed. However, he believed in the vision of the founders that electric cars do not have to be unattractive. He also got involved in the design of the cars themselves. In short, because he believed in the idea, he at least give it a try even though the most likely outcome was failure.

6. Focus on signal over noise

He believes that companies should be able to distinguish which efforts directly contribute to the betterment of a product, and which efforts do not. Once people have identified which ones are contributing to a better product, they should focus on that.

Efforts that do not necessarily make a product better are considered noise and should be stopped.

7. Look for problem solvers

Elon recommends looking for the problem solvers. To know who these people are, he asks questions like how they solved their particular problems several layers down. He believes that the people who are able to describe what happened up to the deepest level are the ones who were really involved in solving the problem. Otherwise, those who were not really involved would not be able to answer to the fullest extent.

8. Attract great people

A company is just a group of people, according to Elon Musk. The most important thing in building or joining a company is to attract great people and to be with them. He believes that the success of a company is largely determined by how talented, hardworking, and focused cohesively in a good direction the people involved are in creating a great product.

9. Have a great product

He advises that in whatever people are doing, they should have a great product or service, with emphasis on great. In offering a product or service in a market where there are existing competitors, the product should be much, much better than the others. It cannot be just a little or slightly better. Otherwise, the consumers will prefer the trusted or familiar brand.

10. Work super hard

When starting a company, Elon warns that people should be ready to work 'super hard'. From his own experience, he describes 'super hard' as working hard every waking hour, every day, seven days a week for a time, especially when he was initially starting out. He made sacrifices against comfortable living in order to put the resources in aid of his business goals. He believes that the people who work doubly hard will, in the end, get twice the work done.

11. Don't fear failure

In an interview, Musk stated that he originally thought that Tesla would fail.

12. Be ready to learn new skills

Don't let what you don't know stop you from tackling important endeavors.

13. Seek out constructive criticism

One success tip that many people avoid is seeking out criticism.

14. Be unrelentingly optimistic

Elon is known for setting impossible deadlines and making requests of his employees to cut costs by up to 90%. A lot of the time these deadlines fail, but often they succeed.

With the optimism to tackle massive goals, you can often achieve success even if you fall a bit short of your original target.

Challenge yourself to think big and this will often yield big returns. Seeking unreasonable levels of success is a strategy that can lead you to exceptional success.

15. Strive to be significantly better than the competition

Put yourself in the shoes of the consumer, Elon says. "They are going to buy the trusted brand unless there is a big difference." So if you want to set yourself apart from the competition, don't just try to be a bit better. Strive to be significantly better.

16. Start from first principles

Elon explains his thoughts about reasoning up from first principles. Boil things down to the most fundamental truths. Reason up from there.

17. Be extremely tenacious

The determination to keep going when the going gets tough is what saved SpaceX and Tesla when both were on the verge of bankruptcy.

18. Focus on a high-value pursuit

Focusing on building a business that you are confident will have a high value for others is a strategy that Elon recommends. Being rigorous and real in your self-analysis will help to keep you grounded and on the path to success.

19. Read more

You don't know what you don't know. You realize there are more things out there.

20. Sex sells

Elon knows that sex sells and uses this to his advantage. Every Tesla car has sexual undertones.

21. Invest profits into new businesses

Both times Musk cashed in a company for millions of dollars, he invested at least 45% of his earnings back into a brand new business within the calendar year.

$10 million of the $22 million that Musk made from the sale of Zip2 went to founding X.com (later PayPal).

$100 million out of the $165 million he made from the sale of PayPal went to founding SpaceX.

22. Innovate

Elon has innovated with Tesla to the point where multiple sources are saying that they have created the best car ever.

23. Know your limits

Musk may be the smartest and hardest working entrepreneur of the 21st century but he still only has 24 hours in a day.

24. Have out of this world ambition

Elon's ambition is to colonize Mars as a way to back up the human race. Colonizing Mars is much more than just a business decision for Musk.

25. Improvise

When SpaceX was told to wait to launch rockets in the U.S, he went and found a Pacific island that he could use straight away. When Tesla needed to test a prototype in the cold, he hired an ice-cream truck with a big refrigerated trailer. Where there is a will, there is often a way when you are willing to improvise and make things work.

26. Create a world-class work environment

Most car factories are dark and gloomy. Tesla takes a different approach. The Tesla factory was inspired by the SpaceX work environment and features light paint and lots of natural light.

27. Let your imagination soar

With awe-inspiring ideas which aim to transform today into future, this innovator has enjoyed a first-mover advantage in all of his business ventures.

28. Focus

Although any investor will tell you that diversity in a portfolio is key, Elon has created billions of dollars in growth by focusing his investments and then exercising control to accelerate the growth further.

29. Constantly improve

Elon said that the single best piece of advice he can give is to constantly think about how you can be doing things better.

30. Start with a premium product

Start by creating desire by offering a premium product to the affluent.

This is the strategy that Musk developed with Tesla when they decided to create the high-end luxury Tesla roadster.

People who are successful today, such as Elon Musk, did not rise to the world spotlight because of uninterrupted triumphs. They have all experienced setbacks, but they were resilient enough to get back up and try again. In fact, they tried many times, and in the process, they learned many things. These thirty rules are not the only rules for success, but we can hope that learning ten more things will help get you on your way.

CHAPTER FIVE

DIFFERENT INVESTMENTS AND NET WORTH

DIFFERENT INVESTMENTS

An abbreviated list of Musk's best investments includes PayPal Holdings, Inc. (NASDAQ: PYPL), SpaceX, DeepMind (NASDAQ: GOOGL), Zip2 Corporation, Tesla, and The Boring Company.

1. PayPal

A short list of PayPal's investors and executives reads like a who's who list of the modern tech industry. The popular online payment system was co-founded by, among others, Ken Howery, Max Levchin, Peter Thiel, and Musk. John Donahoe, who also works on the boards of eBay and Intel, serves as the chairman for PayPal.

Musk no longer holds a stake in PYPL, having exited his position after eBay purchased the company for $1.5 billion's worth of stock in 2002. Something that Carl Icahn helped undo more than a decade later.

Musk reportedly earned between $165 million and $175 million for his part. Not a bad return on the $10 million that Musk used to co-found X.com, the precursor to PayPal.

2. SpaceX

As he has done with the proceeds from prior corporate acquisitions, Musk used most of his PayPal fortune to found the Space Exploration Technologies Corporation, more commonly known as SpaceX. By most accounts, Musk sank $100+ million to get SpaceX off the ground in 2002.

The company has been a remarkable success, both financially and technologically. NASA awarded SpaceX with a lucrative contract in 2006. It launched Falcon 1, the first-ever private liquid-propellant rocket to reach orbit, in 2008. Two years later, the Dragon spacecraft actually reached the International Space Station (ISS). In 2011, NASA granted SpaceX a second contract to help shuttle crew between the ISS and Earth.

As a private company, SpaceX is more difficult to value than PayPal. However, in August 2017 private financing put the company's worth around $21.5 billion.

Musk still owns a controlling interest, which means that his share is worth far more than the $100 million that he originally invested. Expect Musk to earn a huge sum if SpaceX is ever taken public.

SpaceX has made space travel exciting again, and Musk is very open on social media with the company's efforts to push space science forward, like landing a rocket upright onto a landing pad in the middle of the Atlantic Ocean. In December 2017, SpaceX successfully landed 19 rockets, which they plan to reuse on future missions. Musk has also made clear his intentions to take humans to Mars by 2024.

3. Zip2 corporation

Zip2 Corporation was an online directory for newspapers and other media. Eventually, Musk added a feature that created the first online Yellow Pages. Within four years, Musk sold Zip2 to Compaq for more than $300 million. Musk immediately used $10 million of his new fortune to create X.com, which became PayPal.

4. DeepMind technologies

Musk struck buyout gold again with his artificial intelligence company DeepMind Technologies. The company launched in late 2010 with Musk as one of the key angel investors. The company would eventually sell to Google for an unconfirmed amount, but most reports put the value between $400 and $600 million

Musk is famously worried about artificial intelligence overtaking humans and invested in DeepMind not to make money, but, as he said to Vanity Fair, "to give me visibility into the rate at which it was developing." Musk has said that what he learned from gaining that visibility was enough to change his way of thinking about all of his ventures, including furthering his plans to colonize Mars in case humans need to escape Earth due to a robot uprising. Yes, this is a real thing that Elon Musk is worried about.

5. Tesla Motors

In November 2017, Tesla announced the creation of fully electric semi-trucks, which are set to hit the road in 2019.

These semis have already seen huge pre-orders from companies such as UPS, PepsiCo, and more. Tesla also produces the sporty Model S, the Model X SUV, the upcoming Model 3 sedan, and the high-end Roadster supercar.

6. The Boring Company

Musk founded the tunnel construction "Boring Company" in late 2016. The basic idea behind The Boring Company is that traffic is awful, and why travel above ground when there's miles and miles of unused earth beneath us? The goal of The Boring Company is to reduce the cost of tunneling while also speeding up production. The Boring Company hopes to achieve this by making smaller tunnels and juicing up the power of Boring Machines.

Musk has hopes that The Boring Company, which has projects in various states in Los Angeles, Hawthorne, the East Coast, and Chicago, will be the key to unlocking hyperloop travel, one of Musk's passions. To fund the project, Musk did what any entrepreneur would do; he started selling hats. On December 16, 2017, Musk announced that he had sold 42,000 Boring Company hats and raised $840,000. The Boring Company is currently burrowing beneath LA to create a 6.5 mile concept tunnel. If the tunnel gets government approval, Musk can go full steam ahead and tunnel away.

NET WORTH

Elon Musk has an estimated net worth of $20.1 billion, making him the 80th richest person in the world according to Forbes.

His fortune owes much to his stake in Tesla Motors Inc. (TSLA), of which he remains CEO and chief product architect. As of December 2017, his net worth was up more than $7 billion from $13.2 billion in March 2016.

SpaceX has also contributed heavily to Musk's net worth. The space-exploration company he founded in 2002 raised $1 billion from Google Inc., and Fidelity Investments in January 2015. According to Forbes, SpaceX is valued at more than $20 billion as of December 2017. Some reports say that Musk owns the same percentage of SpaceX as he does of SolarCity and Tesla, where his stakes are in the 20 to 30% range.

Musk is also a generous philanthropist through the Musk Foundation, which he chairs. The foundation focuses on delivering solar energy systems to parts of the world that have been struck by natural disasters. It collaborated with SolarCity to bring a 25 kW solar power system to Coden, Alabama after the area had been hit by a hurricane in 2010. After Sōma, Japan was badly damaged by a tsunami in 2011, the foundation donated $250,000 towards a solar power project.

CHAPTER SIX

IDEAS/TAKE ON ARTIFICIAL INTELLIGENCE

Musk's alarming views on the dangers of A.I. first went viral after he spoke at M.I.T. in 2014—speculating (pre-Trump) that A.I. was probably humanity's biggest existential threat. He added that he was increasingly inclined to think there should be some national or international regulatory oversight—anathema to Silicon Valley— to make sure that we don't do something very foolish. He went on to state that with artificial intelligence, we are summoning the demon. You know all of those stories where there is the guy with the pentagram, the holy water and he's like, yeah, he's sure he can control the demon? Doesn't work out. Some A.I. engineers have found Musk's theatricality so absurdly amusing that they began echoing it.

The AI technologies of today are simply not advanced enough or sufficiently embedded into our society for that to happen. But in the long term, the outlook is less clear. AI technologies are developing fast and so are their attendant risks.

AI applied to warfare and policing is certainly a concern. Autonomous armed robots, which can track and target people using facial recognition software, are just around the corner. Let loose, such machines would keep on killing until they ran out of targets or ammunition. This reminds us that AI has no social awareness, conscience, mercy, or remorse. It simply does what it has been trained to do.

The Terminator Scenario is a real possibility, but it's something that we can easily foresee and develop measures to protect ourselves against via legislation and in how we design robot intelligence. Arguably the greater threat from AI comes from developing machines that are better decision makers than we are.

As a consequence, we could become the slaves of automated decision-makers and whoever controls them.

This may seem like a futuristic nightmare, but it is an insidious creeping process that is well underway. AI-based systems are beginning to replace or enhance many white-collar jobs that are currently done by human experts.

This is because AI can interpret situations and make better calls than humans in those jobs. For example, AI machines are better at spotting the signs of cancer on a medical scan than the best radiologists.

Many of our key life choices on social media and shopping sites are influenced by AI. Algorithms determine what content we see on our News Feed and recommend who we should or shouldn't date. People don't set your insurance premiums anymore, and if you can't get a loan, it is because an AI-based system denied it. Many companies are using AI to screen job applicants for roles. In a few decades, it may be that our lives are so controlled that we find ourselves unable to deviate from the life path that AI decides—we will be slaves to a machine-determined future.

What makes this scenario so dangerous is that it isn't being planned by some overarching master intelligence or machine overlord. We are creating the very technology that could lead to our own demise. This makes AI difficult to protect against or control. Instead, machines would take over in a piecemeal fashion. Whether it arrives today or in decades, the threat posed by AI is real.

CHAPTER SEVEN

POLITICAL AND WORLD VIEW

Elon Musk has a lot to say. He is seldom at a loss for words when it comes to promoting his ideas for pollution-free transportation, space exploration or battery storage. He has been known to weigh in on other technologies, such as when he famously referred to hydrogen fuel cells as "fool cells."

What do we know about Elon Musk and politics? Not much. Since 2003, he has donated $258,350 to Democratic candidates and $261,300 to Republicans. You can't get much more even-handed than that. During the last election cycle, he gave money to both Democratic President Barack Obama and current Republican presidential candidate, Senator Lindsey Graham.

There is a difference between personal contributions and corporate donations. The companies that Musk controls, like Tesla, SolarCity, and SpaceX, all make it a point to support candidates who will assist them in navigating local politics successfully.

Tesla is locked in a nationwide fight to get permission to market its cars directly to consumers in several states, bypassing traditional dealers.

That campaign is going slowly and has suffered some high profile setbacks, most notably in Texas. That state's legislature only meets once every 2 years and handed Tesla a stinging rebuke at the end of the last session in June when it refused to approve an amendment to its dealer franchise laws, even after Musk personally traveled to Austin to lobby state legislators.

SolarCity has a running feud with several entrenched utility companies who feel threatened by the idea of rooftop solar power. The argument is couched in terms of protecting customers who don't have a solar system, but in reality, the utilities are used to being in control of every aspect of the electricity generating business and fear to lose any of that control.

Of course, Musk's companies are going to support politicians who will support their business objectives.

But even there, the amount of corporate contributions have been a fraction of what other companies donate. SpaceX's official PAC has contributed $90,577 to candidates during the current election cycle, while Boeing donated $687,000.

Some people think of Musk, with his all-encompassing worldview and passion for solving humanities problems, as a liberal. Others think that he must be a libertarian because his businesses often run into opposition from regulators. For instance, transportation officials in California are currently moving slowly to address the matter of self-driving cars on public roads. Tesla is ready to run with its autonomous Autopilot suite of sensors, scanners, and software and is anxious for the regulators to catch up to its vision.

Tesla received a crucial government loan early in its existence that helped it get started. It later repaid the loan in full ahead of schedule. SpaceX works closely with NASA so that both can thrive. It appears that Musk is no Reaganite.

On the other hand, he pulled his support for FWD.us, an organization founded by Facebook founder Mark Zuckerberg to promote immigration reform.

Musk, himself a naturalized US citizen, supported the group's goals but not its methods. In order to cozy up to conservative members of Congress who oppose immigration reform, the group took out campaign ads promoting items on the conservative agenda, including drilling in the Arctic. Musk bailed at that point. Later, he said the following at an All Things Digital conference: "Initially, I agreed to be a part of FWD.us because I agree with immigration reform. But I think the methods that were employed – it was a little too Kissinger-esque, Realpolitik. I think we should try to make things happen for the right reason. We shouldn't give in to the politics. If we give in to that, we'll get the political system we deserve."

What does that tell us about Musk's political beliefs? Not much. It is just about the only insight that we have from a man who is famously eloquent on so many subjects – except politics.

CONCLUSION

Do you have a product or service that the market doesn't seem to understand or value? Are you met with skepticism? Are you too far ahead of the curve to be mainstream yet?

Take a lesson from the Tesla. Musk's business plan had three steps. First, was to develop a high-end, high-performance sports car proving that electric vehicles were both cool and feasible. Second, he rolled out a luxury sedan to compete with the likes of BMW and Mercedes. The third leg of his plan was to produce low-cost electric vehicles for the masses.

Most of us, especially in small businesses, go for the safety of numbers. We start with the masses. We create new products and services that are low-cost and often kind of 'vanilla'. We believe that if we get them into the hands of a lot of people, then success will be assured.

Here is the problem that Musk saw with this approach. When something is different, the masses are cautious and often suspicious. They sit back and wait because they aren't risk takers. They want social proof and they want their neighbors to do the proving. Once it becomes mainstream, then they jump in.

Any new idea need people who think outside of the box and quite frankly, who enjoy being different and the status that is attached to that. They WANT to stand out from the crowd. They set the trends and eventually everyone wants what they have. This is the trickledown effect.

Musk knows that one of the 'rules' of the automobile business is that high-end luxury options enjoy the trickledown effect. By starting at the top end of the market rather than with economy cars as other manufacturers are doing, he tapped into the way that humans are wired.

Other companies struggled to get the new-fangled idea of electric vehicle accepted by the mass market. The mass market resisted because they aren't the risk-takers that needed to be targeted. They want a proven concept.

Tesla narrowed his focus to the luxury market by fulfilling the demand for performance and good looks. And oh, by the way, these sleek, sexy cars just happen to be powered by electricity. Now everyone is paying attention.

So how does this apply to you and your small business? Aim for the top end of your respective market. Narrow your niche. Add value to your offerings. Become the premium product. Talk to people who are looking for value, not the lowest prices.

When you become the premium product in your market, you work less but make more. Because demand trickles down, the cautious folks who wouldn't talk to you before will get their social proof.

Printed in Great Britain
by Amazon